Sarah Jane Dickenson is a writer and academic. Her work has been produced in a variety of settings from theatres, sports venues, community centres, schools and prisons, working extensively with large and small casts in participatory and community settings. She has worked most recently with Graeae Theatre Company, the Goethe Institute and The Wellcome Trust. Her latest plays to go into print are *CBA* and *That Berlin Moment*, both published by Barbican Press. She is currently Head of the Department of English, Creative Writing and American Studies at the University of Hull.

REF!

by

Sarah Jane Dickenson

BARB ICAN PRESS

First published in Great Britain by
Barbican Press in 2019

Copyright © Sarah Jane Dickenson, 2019

The right of Sarah Janes Dickenson to be identified
as the author of this book has been asserted
by her in accordance with sections 77 and 78
of the Copyright, Designs and Patents Act, 1988.

Barbican Press: Hull and London
Registered office: 1 Ashenden Road, E5 0DP

www.barbicanpress.com
@barbicanpress1

Cover by Rawshock Design
Cover Image: Alan Poulson/Dreamstime.com

A CIP catalogue for this book is available from the British Library

ISBN: 978-1-909954-37-3

Typeset by Imprint Press

Printed in England by CPI Group (UK) Ltd.

for my mother

Foreword

I was at an exhibition for Rugby League when a woman came up to me and said, 'Are you the woman who refereed men's League matches?'

'Yes,' I said.

'I want to write a play about you.'

'Oh, right,' I said, looking over her head for another glass of red and an escape. She gave me her card and eventually I gave her my email and I didn't think any more about it.

After a flurry of emails from her I replied and reluctantly agreed to meet for a coffee and cake. Needless to say, I was sceptical. I was working for The Rugby Football League (RFL) at the time, sorting the Referee Training Programme amongst other things, and I'd not long come off of the back of sorting the Festival of World Cups. I was trying to make changes, a difference. Did I have time for this? Also, and most importantly, did I want to share parts of my story that were, well... ?

So, before we met, I was rehearsing how to let her down gently - or not so gently. We tell it as it is in Hull. But at the start of the meeting she - Sarah Jane - said, 'This play isn't you.'

'Excuse me?' I said, surprised that I felt a little bit miffed.

'It's going to be inspired by your story. And then it's going to inspire other women, young and old.'

'To be referees?' I asked. (Not many had followed me into refereeing the men's game.)

'To do anything they want to do. To know their stories are important, and know they can make things happen.'

'How many plays have you written?' I asked. I mean, I hadn't exactly seen her name up in lights in the West End. Turns out she had a track record for working with people who never thought folk would want to hear from the likes of them. In Britain but overseas too, Sarah Jane got close to these people. She helped them share their stories by turning them into plays. The best plays possible. When people see their stories on stage, they start to believe they can bring about change.

Why hadn't I heard of this?

We had several more meetings, always over coffee and cake.

We talked, she wrote some script, I read it, we talked some more, she wrote some more. I began to see what she was doing. I didn't want my family to feel exposed so I shared it with them and explained how the play was 'inspired by' my story and they got it – a bit quicker than me to be honest.

It wasn't a short process; it took me quite a while to share certain difficult moments in my life. For me the breakthrough came when I took Sarah Jane to see her first live League match. It was then she realised how I really felt about the game, how those around us felt. And I started to feel that maybe, just maybe this play would have helped my younger self.

So, we had more coffee and more cake and I kept talking and she kept writing.

One day I caught up with Rod Dixon, Artistic Director of Red Ladder Theatre Company. Our paths had crossed before when the RFL supported a play Red Ladder directed and produced. Rod told me about Space2. This organization takes projects like our play and develops them as a way of engaging communities and building on their strengths. Generously Rod organised a script-in-hand reading of REF! and invited along the Directors of Space2, Dawn Fuller and Emma Tregidden. After the reading it was clear they could see the potential in the play but more importantly for me, we all 'got on'.

So, we arranged to go for coffee and cake.

Working with Emma, Dawn and Sarah Jane it was clear we wanted the play to be a catalyst for women in the Rugby League community to share their stories. So Space2 produced the play and a SMART (Social Museum and Art) gallery. SMART Gallery is the brain-child of artist Helen Peyton, who was long-listed for the Turner Prize in 2015 and joined our project. Years with Rugby League gifted women with memories and souvenirs, which have become the SMART gallery that travels to clubs and appears on-line.

With this structure in place the play was toured to rugby league clubs, and performed in their bars or shared spaces. The impact of the first tour of the play was amazing, way beyond our expectations. I can't tell you how many women came forward, wanting to tell their stories, but also how many of them said, 'I didn't think my story was important.' Word of mouth meant more clubs and theatres wanted the play so we extended the tour. After the play premiered, I found myself on TV, radio, in the paper, in demand as an inspirational speaker, MC and even pulling balls out of the bag for the Women's Challenge Cup Semi Final draw.

And still it goes on. As I write, the play has been invited to be performed in the House of Commons, and a tour is planned to support the forthcoming Rugby League World Cups 2021 (RLWC2021). We are looking to take the play to the southern hemisphere, where Rugby League is popular or emerging. What's more, the stories we have gathered so far will have a permanent home in the Museum of Rugby League in Bradford.

As you read this play, who knows, a whole new act might start to write itself. Your life might change. That's what has happened to me.

During the playmaking process, I too made a change. I was inspired to make positive differences in a more direct way for young women. I took the plunge and set up my own company, Common Sense Initiatives (CSI), which is going from strength to strength.

So, if a woman pops up and says I want to write a play about you, bob on and go for that coffee and cake.

Julia Lee
Former Rugby League Referee and
Director of CSI

Acknowledgements

I would like to thank: Dawn Fuller, Emma Tregidden, Andy Lee, Liz Barker, Helen Payton, Frances Murray-Fuentes, Rod Dixon, Will Tristram, Carolyn Eden, Emma Leah Golding, Lee Bainbridge, Leanne Rowley, Lee Toomes, Emma Louise James, Marlon James, Ed Heaton, Sally Brown, Olivia Parham.

Hull KR, Batley Bull Dogs, Featherstone Rovers, The University of Hull, Space2, CSI, Christmas TV and Film, Red Ladder Theatre, Interplay Theatre, Arts Council England, The National Lottery Heritage Fund.

Special thanks to Julia Lee for being brave enough to share her story, and more importantly for being willing to have it adapted. And to the women involved in Rugby League who, after seeing the play, wanted to share their stories.

The play can be performed in two ways.
It can be performed just as ACT ONE.
Or it can be played in its entirety.

CHARACTERS

(The play can be performed by a minimum of four actors, 2 women and 2 men with the men taking multiple roles.)

In order of appearance

Alex
Touch Judge
Touch Judge 2
Jean (Alex's Mum)
Uncle Mike
Chairman Doug Fletcher

In London

Simon
Wigan Bloke

In Australia

Kev Kopec
Steve Morrow club captain

ACT ONE

SCENE 1

1990. CUPBOARD AT THE RUGBY CLUB
IT IS SERVING AS ALEX'S
CHANGING ROOM

(ALEX is hemmed in by mops, buckets and brooms. She is wearing a parka coat and sitting on a makeshift seat. She stares ahead then starts to weep silently. The weeping gets worse but always it is silent. It builds to be the snotty wailing of a lost child, but always silent.

There is a knock at the door. Alex wipes her nose on her sleeve and starts to get changed. She really doesn't have enough space)

ALEX

When am I going to feel bloody worth it?

(Enter TOUCH JUDGES)

TOUCH JUDGE

Alex? Are you in there?

(Alex nods and silently mouths the word 'yes'. She is trying to gather herself)

TOUCH JUDGE (CONT'D)

Alex? Are you ready?

(Alex silently mouths the word 'no' and starts weeping again)

TOUCH JUDGE (CONT'D)

Alex? *(Knocking)* Alex? It's time.

(Alex mouths 'no, no, no')

TOUCH JUDGE 2

Is she ready?

TOUCH JUDGE

Can't hear a thing.

                    TOUCH JUDGE 2
Everyone else is ready.

                    TOUCH JUDGE
You worked with her before?

                    TOUCH JUDGE 2
No. You?

                    TOUCH JUDGE
You worked with a woman ref before?

                    TOUCH JUDGE 2
Blimey, you telling me there's more than one?

                    TOUCH JUDGE
Only a couple, thank Christ.

                    TOUCH JUDGE 2
I've heard she's a bit...

                    TOUCH JUDGE
A bit what?

                    TOUCH JUDGE 2
A bit... you know.

                    TOUCH JUDGE
Who said that?

                    TOUCH JUDGE 2
You know... people.

                    TOUCH JUDGE
What they say then?

                    TOUCH JUDGE 2
I dunno, they just said she's a bit...

                    TOUCH JUDGE
Oh right! That's all we need, a woman who's a bit...!

TOUCH JUDGE 2

I know!

TOUCH JUDGE

This is not the game for a bleeding experiment. Have you heard that lot out there? I mean, this is bloody Filey!

TOUCH JUDGE 2

And a derby! We'll be lucky if we get out in one piece. Mind you... I heard she drinks pints.

TOUCH JUDGE

So. Couple of pints don't make a ref.

TOUCH JUDGE 2

She drank Parham under the table.

TOUCH JUDGE

Parham? Steve Parham?

TOUCH JUDGE 2

He's a legend!

TOUCH JUDGE

Eh, he only beat me when we went on to double chasers. I'd gone twenty pints with him, straight after match.

TOUCH JUDGE 2

They went on to double chasers.

TOUCH JUDGE

No!

TOUCH JUDGE 2

I know!

TOUCH JUDGE

Not all bad then.

TOUCH JUDGE 2

Mebe.

TOUCH JUDGE

Just mostly bad

TOUCH JUDGE 2

(Calling through door) Alex. You ready?

(Alex mouths 'No')

TOUCH JUDGE 2 (CONT'D)

Ref! Ref are you ready?

ALEX

Course I'm ready!

(To herself)

(Alex wipes her nose on her sleeve one last time. She stands dressed as a rugby league referee. Braces herself for the game ahead)

TOUCH JUDGE

She bloody crying?

ALEX

(Shouting through door) I'm in a bleeding cupboard! Stinks of bleach, industrial strength. Gets right up my nose! And the glamour of a twenty watt bulb. Can't see a bloody thing. If anything is hanging out that shouldn't be when I step out let me know.

(Alex comes out of the cupboard)

TOUCH JUDGE

Thought our changing room was crap but -

ALEX

You decided on your side?

TOUCH JUDGE 2

I lost. I'm home side to start.

ALEX

Poor you.

TOUCH JUDGE 2

I know. Filey fans are psycho at the best of times -

ALEX/TOUCH JUDGE/TOUCH JUDGE 2

But always in the first half.

ALEX

Glad I'm in the middle then.

TOUCH JUDGE

If I remember rightly last time we got covered in a serious amount of gob.

ALEX

Bet that was just the women.
Don't worry, any daft stuff will go straight in my report. If I can't protect my touch judges... you up for a pint afterwards?

TOUCH JUDGE

Did you really drink Parham under the table...

ALEX

Haven't you heard? How to hold a skin-full is standard ref training now. So I'll be at Crown and first round is on me. Right then.

(Alex gets her watch, notebook etc together)

Watches?

TOUCH JUDGE/TOUCH JUDGE 2

Watches.

ALEX

Flags?

TOUCH JUDGE/TOUCH JUDGE 2

Flags.

ALEX

(Checking) Cards, and...

TOUCH JUDGE 2

And bigger balls than a pawnbrokers! *(Beat)* Well. I mean -

ALEX

Bigger balls? Sorry no. But will a diamond studded vagina do?

TOUCH JUDGE

Oh Christ she's a punk!

ALEX

I lied about the diamonds - it's just tattooed with 'I love rugby league' smiley face.

TOUCH JUDGE 2

Is it?

ALEX

Daft bugger. Right. We're on.

(She braces herself. The crowd are more than noisy – eg - 'Why aren't you at home putting in the Yorkshires's! / Can't you cook that why you here! / We've waited all season for a good ref another week won't matter!')

SCENE 2

1980s. JEAN'S TERRACED HOUSE
LIVING ROOM

(There are a few small photos of family around. Alex is bouncing on the settee. JEAN is busy doing something)

ALEX

Gymnast. See Mum, see, gymnast? They finish like this.
Could be a gymnast me.

JEAN

Have you seen your brother's uniform?

ALEX

Which bit?

JEAN

All of it. I've yours, look at the state!

ALEX

I'll do a somersault Mum, like a gymnast.

JEAN

You won't.

ALEX

I do them on your bed.

JEAN

Then don't!

ALEX

(Bouncing. Looking at picture) This me Aunty Joan?

JEAN

How can you see bouncing?

ALEX

I could be a rugby league forward, scoring a try, see mum, see? *(Dives on sofa)* What she die of?

                    JEAN

Heart.

                    ALEX

How old was she?

                    JEAN

Forty four. Here's your brother's - you see his is really clean.

                    ALEX

That Uncle Jim?

                    JEAN

You know it is. It's like he hasn't...

                    ALEX

What he die of?

                    JEAN

Heart.

                    ALEX

How old was he?

                    JEAN

Forty two.

                    ALEX

I could be in a circus. *(Balancing)* See. Trapeze artist me, see Mum, see?

                    JEAN

What's this on your pumps?

                    ALEX

You know Dad?

                    JEAN

Did you wear them outside?

                    ALEX

Photos Mum?

JEAN

Did you?

ALEX

Mebe.

JEAN

I've told you not to -

ALEX

There aren't photos of him.

JEAN

There are.

ALEX

Not out.
Where Mum?

JEAN

I'm busy.

ALEX

I'll look.

JEAN

You'll make a mess.

ALEX

Won't. Promise.

JEAN

Look Alex I'm trying to - before I go to work.

ALEX

I can't remember what he looks like. In games today I thought, I can't
remember.

JEAN

You were three. You can't expect to remember -

                    ALEX

Steven remembers.

                    JEAN

He was older.

                    ALEX

His face - can't remember. His voice - can't remember. There's a smell - I don't know if it's his. I might remember - if I see a photo.

                    JEAN

(Beat) There's an album.

                    ALEX

Where?

                    JEAN

Somewhere safe.

                    ALEX

You don't know.

                    JEAN

Safe places are difficult to remember.

                    ALEX

I'll look under stairs.

                    JEAN

No. No, look in sideboard. There's a box.

   (Alex looks. Takes out a white box. Jean is busy doing something)

                    ALEX

This posh box?

                    JEAN

That's it.

                    ALEX

Oooh, soft!

JEAN

Was a wedding album in it?

ALEX

You got wedding photos in here?

JEAN

No.

ALEX

(Looking at picture) There's us kids at..?

JEAN

Scarborough. Always Scarborough.

ALEX

Is that him?

JEAN

Uncle Steve.

ALEX

Our Steven named after him?

JEAN

Yes.

ALEX

What he die of?

JEAN

Heart.

ALEX

How old was he?

JEAN

Oh the oldest, he was forty six.

ALEX

How old are you Mum?

JEAN

They're your father's family.
(Taking up clothes) I'm putting these in.

ALEX

I can't find him.

JEAN

He is in there.

ALEX

But where?

JEAN

(Goes over and looks in album. Sorts out a photo) There he is. *(She starts to go)*

ALEX

But Mum?

JEAN

I won't get these dry if -

ALEX

Mum. It's a coffin.

JEAN

Yes. His coffin.

ALEX

But. A coffin?

JEAN

He's in there.

ALEX

Is there no other photo of him?

JEAN

Not in the coffin.

ALEX

Standing up?

JEAN

In the coffin?

ALEX

Standing anywhere.

JEAN

No.

ALEX

Mum?

JEAN

What?

ALEX

What he die of?

JEAN

—

ALEX

Mum? Problems with his heart?

JEAN

You could say that.

(Enter UNCLE MIKE)

UNCLE MIKE

Hiya darl!

(Hugs Alex)

ALEX

You smell funny.

UNCLE MIKE

Eau de bitter - eh Jean - get it - eau de bitter - just a swift one.

ALEX

Uncle Mike! I can do this Uncle Mike! *(Starts bouncing and continues through next section of dialogue)* See Uncle Mike, see? Like Olympics.

UNCLE MIKE

Jean, where's Steve?

JEAN

Sorry Mike, he's out. He doesn't want to go.

UNCLE MIKE

Not go?

ALEX

Go where?

JEAN

Not go.

ALEX

Not go?

UNCLE MIKE

Why not go?

JEAN

Why d'you think?

ALEX

Uncle Mike - Uncle Mike!

UNCLE MIKE

Oi calm down! Where's that Barbie I bought you?

ALEX

Natalia Barbiecov - the famous Romanian gymnast. Pushed herself too high, too far, too often.

UNCLE MIKE

Did she?

ALEX

She did. A fate that often befalls the sportswoman trying to prove she's up there with the men.

UNCLE MIKE

Jean?

JEAN

Next door dog chewed her leg off.

UNCLE MIKE

Why didn't you just brush her hair like every other girl?

ALEX

I don't like dolls.

UNCLE MIKE

(To Jean) She doesn't like dolls?

JEAN

No.

ALEX

Never.

UNCLE MIKE

Never?

JEAN

Never.

UNCLE MIKE

Bit scary. What's Steve's problem?

JEAN

He's tried to tell you.

UNCLE MIKE

It's a derby, grudge match.

JEAN

He doesn't enjoy it.

UNCLE MIKE

Watching grown men batter each other, what's not for a bloke to enjoy?

ALEX

Rugby league match?

UNCLE MIKE

You put him off Jean.

JEAN

Me?

UNCLE MIKE

(To Jean) Steve shouldn't forget his Dad. *(To Alex)* He was a great brother, great bloke.

JEAN

They're your memories not theirs.

UNCLE MIKE

(To Alex) He loved you kids to bits. *(Lying)* Always telling me so, remember?

ALEX

I can't remember.

UNCLE MIKE

You can't forget your Dad. You just can't. He wanted Steve to be a copper, like him. Watch league like him.

JEAN

He never took him.

UNCLE MIKE

He wanted to, was busy, he'd want me to sort.

ALEX

Take me.

UNCLE MIKE

—

ALEX

Oh please Uncle Mike, I love seeing battering, please take me, please.

UNCLE MIKE

Jean. You know - season ticket - bloke - son - nephew thing.

ALEX

Steve loves Duran Duran, not sports.

UNCLE MIKE

Duran Duran? Even more reason Steve should...

JEAN

Can't you take her? I thought you have influence.

UNCLE MIKE

I do. I mean, the chairman says I'm indispensable...

ALEX

Please Uncle Mike, please?

JEAN

What exactly do you do at the club Mike?

UNCLE MIKE

Okay this time. But just this time. I'll talk to Steve later Jean, tell him. I want a word. *(To Alex)* Get sorted then.

ALEX

Yay!

JEAN

You'll need to wrap up warm mind. Get gloves and hat.

UNCLE MIKE

No need. I'll get her some there.

JEAN

Influence?

UNCLE MIKE

I get discount.

ALEX

Rovers 'til we die!

SCENE 3

1980s STREET

(Alex and Uncle Mike are waiting for a bus)

ALEX

That was brilliant Uncle Mike, brilliant! Just brilliant!

UNCLE MIKE

Eh. Don't tell your Mum what you were shouting.

ALEX

You said the ref was fucking blind - I just agreed.

UNCLE MIKE

Okay don't tell her what we was shouting.

ALEX

Can I go again, can I?

UNCLE MIKE

Your brother. Does he play rugby at school?

ALEX

I told you, he hates sports.

UNCLE MIKE

All of 'em?

ALEX

'Cept dancing.

UNCLE MIKE

School makes boys dance?

ALEX

Did you feel the crowd, did ya?
Like one big heaving beast.

UNCLE MIKE

Only when that ref stuffed up.

ALEX

I felt like I was part of this animal - the crowd, the players - that was strong and fierce, but calm. And nobody, nothing could... and I was part of it, I felt safe, really safe and special... but when that player of theirs got injured - everyone - we were all bothered - all cared.

UNCLE MIKE

Yeh, we did. But when he picked himself up - carried on - he got battered again and we cheered like mad.

Time for a pint.

You want some pop? Crisps? If you're good you can have a taste of my pint.

ALEX

Can I?

UNCLE MIKE

You can if you don't tell your Mum.

ALEX

Watching it, I couldn't keep still

UNCLE MIKE

I noticed. So did rest of row.

ALEX

I want to get out there, get on the pitch.

UNCLE MIKE

You can't.

ALEX

Why not? I'm good at every sport at school. I bet I can do league.

UNCLE MIKE

Girls, ladies, don't play rugby league. No girls teams see.

ALEX

Aren't there?

UNCLE MIKE

Not round here.

ALEX

That's not fair!

UNCLE MIKE

Yeh, I know. 'Cos if there was, darl, with my influence, I'd take you right along, get you right in there.

ALEX

Would ya?

UNCLE MIKE

(Lying) Course

ALEX

I really, really want to be out there in the middle of that heaving bunch of... And I will, somehow I will.

UNCLE MIKE

Does Steven really hate sports?

ALEX

It's not just sports they get him for. It's other stuff.

UNCLE MIKE

What other stuff?

ALEX

All other stuff. The way he talks, the way he walks, wears his uniform, does his hair...

UNCLE MIKE

What he want to do that for? Why'd he want to stand out like that? He should keep his head down, play sport.

ALEX

But he doesn't like sport.

UNCLE MIKE

Then he should pretend. Pretend he likes sport, wear an Adidas trackie top, get the hairspray out his hair, why's he making such a fuss? He should fit in, just fit in. Why'd he want to get above himself.

ALEX

He has bruises. Marks.

UNCLE MIKE

(Beat) He has... He has to... stand on his own two... you know.

ALEX

I thought telling you... you'd want to sort it.

UNCLE MIKE

Look, if you want the season ticket.

ALEX

Me?

UNCLE MIKE

You.

ALEX

But, what about Steve?

UNCLE MIKE

I'm only asking once, you want the ticket or not.

ALEX

—

UNCLE MIKE

Well do ya?

ALEX

Please!

UNCLE MIKE

Sorted.

SCENE 4

RUGBY GROUND 1990s NORTH OF ENGLAND

(Alex is standing between two rugby captains. Ready to toss a coin and start a match)

ALEX

Afternoon lads.

CAPTAINS

Ref.

ALEX

Understand this is a grudge match.

CAPTAIN

Grudge match?

CAPTAIN 2

Not a grudge match Ref.

ALEX

No?

CAPTAINS

No.

ALEX

What then?

CAPTAIN

Hate.

CAPTAIN 2

Yeh, hate.

ALEX

A hate match?

CAPTAINS

Yeh.

                    ALEX

Right. Well -

                    CAPTAIN

Professional hate, mind you.

                    CAPTAIN 2

Yeh, professional. Always professional.

                    ALEX

That's alright then.

                    CAPTAIN

You ref Filey last week?

                    ALEX

I did.

                    CAPTAIN 2

I 'eard.

                    CAPTAIN

Yeh. I 'eard.

                    ALEX

Heads or tails?

                    CAPTAIN

Their hate ain't professional.

                    CAPTAIN 2

T'aint.

                    CAPTAIN

Being that they're wankers.

                    CAPTAIN 2

Complete bloody wankers.
Heard you did a fierce job.

                    CAPTAIN

But fair.

CAPTAIN 2

Yeh, fair.

(Rugby player off)

PLAYER

Oh bollocks! We got a woman in the middle.

CAPTAIN

Oi! She did Filey last week.

PLAYER

Oh bollocks! That her?

CAPTAIN 2

Her is 'Ref' to you.
And we'll have no buggering swearing!

CAPTAIN

(To his own team) Goes for you buggers too.

ALEX

Buggering heads or buggering tails?

CAPTAIN

Heads Ref.

CAPTAIN 2

Tails Ref.

ALEX

Sorted.

(She tosses a coin)

SCENE 5

1980s RUGBY CLUB

(Uncle Mike is sweeping/tidying. Enter CHAIRMAN DOUG)

CHAIRMAN DOUG

Ah, Mike this is where you're hiding.

UNCLE MIKE

Chairman.

CHAIRMAN DOUG

Please Mike, you've been around this club a long time, always willing, part of the fabric, don't bother with 'Chairman'.

UNCLE MIKE

Oh, right.

CHAIRMAN DOUG

Boss is fine.

UNCLE MIKE

Boss.

CHAIRMAN DOUG

Cleaner off?

UNCLE MIKE

You told her you didn't need two receptionists.

CHAIRMAN DOUG

We don't. Size and shape Mike, size and shape, always chasing that commercial waistline.

UNCLE MIKE

The cleaner, she was one of the two receptionists, she also worked the turnstiles and was the maker of the sausage rolls with the pig tails for the hospitality boxes.

CHAIRMAN DOUG

With the pig tails?

UNCLE MIKE

With the pig tails.

CHAIRMAN DOUG

I love the pigs tails!
Why didn't she say?

UNCLE MIKE

—

CHAIRMAN DOUG

To be honest Mike, the number of businesses I've had, once you've seen one receptionist...

Anyway, you're doing a great job Mike, great job.

UNCLE MIKE

Thanks boss but long term...?

CHAIRMAN DOUG

You been drinking Mike?

UNCLE MIKE

Celebrating the win Boss.

CHAIRMAN DOUG

That was yesterday.

UNCLE MIKE

It's past 5 o'clock

CHAIRMAN DOUG

So?

UNCLE MIKE

What man in this city hasn't had a drink past 5 o'clock.

CHAIRMAN DOUG

The toilets been done?

UNCLE MIKE

Toilets? Me?

CHAIRMAN DOUG

With the cleaner gone...

UNCLE MIKE

But I thought one of the women volunteers...

CHAIRMAN DOUG

You're a volunteer.

UNCLE MIKE

A volunteer? But I thought -

CHAIRMAN DOUG

You thought what Mike?

UNCLE MIKE

I thought I was... a bit more.

CHAIRMAN DOUG

You are Mike, you are. I've bunged you the odd tenner and I bet that wasn't declared eh Mike? Eh!

UNCLE MIKE

But you said long term -

CHAIRMAN DOUG

I'd love to think long term Mike but with the bitch of a club's finances as they are...

UNCLE MIKE

But you said -

CHAIRMAN DOUG

I can read men. I've made businesses on reading men. And I bet there are no half measures with you Mike, no single shots, no half pints, all or nothing eh?

UNCLE MIKE

What man would be seen dead with a half pint glass?

CHAIRMAN DOUG

Volunteers can turn up pissed Mike, I don't like it but they can. Workers can't.

UNCLE MIKE

I only had one -

CHAIRMAN DOUG

Then you can't hold your drink, which as you know in this city is considered a heinous crime.

UNCLE MIKE

(Quietly) Maybe I had more than one.

CHAIRMAN DOUG

You what? You're mumbling.

UNCLE MIKE

More than one.

CHAIRMAN DOUG

How many is more Mike?

UNCLE MIKE

Only three.

CHAIRMAN DOUG

And the whisky chasers?

UNCLE MIKE

—

CHAIRMAN DOUG

You stink of supermarket whisky.

UNCLE MIKE

I drank them in the pub!
I sweep up, I empty bins, I clean your car, I clean up sick in your car and -

CHAIRMAN DOUG

Eh! My son's sick - and I had a firm word - with his mum.

UNCLE MIKE

Indispensable you said, indispensable!

CHAIRMAN DOUG

Best we take this down a notch or two, as you've been imbibing. Now look Mike, I know you go that extra mile for this club, I know that. And no one appreciates that more than me. If you're there for the club... Look I'll be honest with you Mike. We're fire fighting, fire fighting. Bottom line is we're near the bottom line. We need more sponsors - funding - initiatives - there are moments of light like the Sports Funded Referee Society Training Scheme which for a few bob I kindly let them avail themselves of the club facilities. Which I'm only too happy to do but you see the real money comes the more we recruit and they are not exactly beating a path to the door. It seems no bugger wants to train to be a referee. Unless you can think of something that gives us an edge in recruiting to the scheme - something a bit special - or even some bugger signing up who isn't a weedy spotty Herbert - but something a bit - you know - different.

UNCLE MIKE

Hang on - I've got one.

CHAIRMAN DOUG

Got what?

UNCLE MIKE

A special new recruit. For your Referee Training Scheme.

CHAIRMAN DOUG

They're supposed to pass a fitness test.

UNCLE MIKE

Fit as a butcher's dog is Alex - Al.

CHAIRMAN DOUG

How'd you know this Al?

UNCLE MIKE

My dead brother's kid. Old enough, brilliant at any sport.
I got Alex a season ticket.

CHAIRMAN DOUG

You did?

UNCLE MIKE

My dead brother couldn't bring the kid.

CHAIRMAN DOUG

Well no.

UNCLE MIKE

We've been coming for years now.
My sister-in-law was in pieces, so I sorted. If it wasn't for me sorting -

CHAIRMAN DOUG

A season ticket holder eh.

UNCLE MIKE

Alex loves the club. Obsessed. Like me. Doesn't play of course...
mother, overprotective, suffocates the kids, always has done since
my brother - a copper - since he died.

CHAIRMAN DOUG

Copper eh. Bet he could hold his drink.

UNCLE MIKE

—

CHAIRMAN DOUG

Season ticket holder eh. See, if they get trained here, in a club they
love, if it gets us a point or two, or five, in a game, in the future, it
will all be worth it. But... *(Pause)*
I've built businesses on instinct Mike.
You know what my instincts are telling me now?

UNCLE MIKE

(Shakes head)

CHAIRMAN DOUG

Screaming it at me.
They're screaming this could be a real defining moment for this all
consuming she-devil of a club, defining.

(MORE)

CHAIRMAN DOUG (CONT'D)

My instincts are never wrong.
Right. Bring Alan in for training.

UNCLE MIKE

The sister in law, she'll want to bring Al herself. Put her foot down I bet.

CHAIRMAN DOUG

One minute in pieces, next putting her foot down, this woman sounds a bit of a nightmare. She going to be trouble?

UNCLE MIKE

She'll just want to say thank you, helping her kid out, very, very grateful I bet.

CHAIRMAN DOUG

We're not a charity Mike. Better be bloody different.
You never know, if this works out, you could be in charge of recruitment to the scheme.

UNCLE MIKE

Really?

CHAIRMAN DOUG

Too important a role for a volunteer that.

UNCLE MIKE

—

(Exit Chairman Doug)

UNCLE MIKE (CONT'D)

Oh... fuck!

SCENE 6

1980s JEAN'S TERRACED HOUSE. LIVING ROOM

(Enter Uncle Mike. He's been drinking. Jean is there, busy)

UNCLE MIKE

Hey! Jean!

JEAN

Mike.

UNCLE MIKE

Is Alex here? You look gorgeous by the way.

JEAN

You look pissed.

UNCLE MIKE

Nope, not pissed, just happy. And you will be happy too when I tell you.

JEAN

When you tell me what?

UNCLE MIKE

Guess. You'll never guess. Go on guess.

JEAN

I don't guess.

UNCLE MIKE

Go on, guess!

JEAN

I don't like surprise parties, hate ghost trains and I'd be a complete spoilsport at Russian roulette so no I'm not guessing.

UNCLE MIKE

I got her in.

JEAN

In? In what?

UNCLE MIKE

Ref training!
I said - to the Chairman, firmly mind - Al wants to be a ref. To the Chairman! A real Chair. But I told him straight so Al's going to be a ref. And she starts on Tuesday. See I sorted!

JEAN

Did you say she?

MIKE

You got any whisky in Jean, to celebrate?

JEAN

Did you say she?

UNCLE MIKE

I said, Alex. Al. That's what she's called isn't it?

JEAN

But not she?

UNCLE MIKE

They'll find out soon enough.

JEAN

And then what Mike?

UNCLE MIKE

I've sorted something, for my brother.

JEAN

They think she's a he. That's not sorting. If they thought she was a she, that would be sorting.

UNCLE MIKE

Yeh and look what you've done to the he.

JEAN

What?

UNCLE MIKE

I've done something good here. Okay it's not the boy but Al's always said if she can't play... Look, it'll be a laugh. I'd love to see his face when she turns up.

JEAN

They'll be laughing at her! You'll have to go back, tell him.

UNCLE MIKE

I'm not doing that.

JEAN

Why? In case you look as stupid as you are.

UNCLE MIKE

Eh. It's up to Al now. They have to - she has to - stand on her own two -

JEAN

I'm not having a child of mine run the risk of being humiliated and bullied - because you lied.

UNCLE MIKE

You really bring a man down Jean. My brother always said you should have been more...

JEAN

More what, Mike?

UNCLE MIKE

Quiet! You're so bloody - no wonder he was always down the pub.

JEAN

But he wasn't always down the pub though was he Mike?

UNCLE MIKE

—

JEAN

He lied to me and you knew.

(Enter Alex. Unnoticed. She's heard a fair bit of the conversation)

(MORE)

JEAN (CONT'D)

When they came to the door, Jeff and Paul, in uniform - instead of the usual CID shiny seated Burtons suits - like that would make a difference to him being dead - but they stood there and they knew - his workmates knew - I mean - he didn't even like Jeff.

When they came to the door, said road accident, over the limit, way over the limit.

UNCLE MIKE

All coppers drink. You're poisoning his memory.

JEAN

I was worried he might have hurt someone else. Worried it was you Mike 'cos he said he was seeing you. I asked - was anyone else hurt? And they looked at each other - in their stupid uniforms that were straining at the buttons and they said no. The woman got out without a scratch. They said she was lucky.

She was a young PC wasn't she Mike? Went onto someone else soon after. Unscathed in more ways than one she was. Bet she hardly remembers. I wish I didn't remember Mike. Wish I had memories like yours.

UNCLE MIKE

I'm going - I don't need to hear this.

(Exit Uncle Mike. Jean notices Alex)

JEAN

How much did you hear?

ALEX

Enough.

JEAN

Oh sweetheart...

ALEX

Was she... The only one.

JEAN

—

ALEX

I had this row - with Steve. I wanted to put something up - in room - his warrant card - Steve said it was an idiot thing to do - I don't remember - I don't remember... was she the only one - was she?

JEAN

No. When he came in smelling of perfume he said it was because he'd arrested someone, had to restrain them.
I was just amazed how many arrests he said he made of petty criminals who drenched themselves in Charlie.

ALEX

I want to do it - the ref training. I'm really fit, I know the rules inside out -

JEAN

They'll think you're getting above yourself -

ALEX

I'll convince them, I'll -

JEAN

They'll laugh at you!

ALEX

Mum, I want in, to be part of the game, the highs, the lows, be part of something really big where the rules are the rules, black and white, and there's nothing to make me feel so... empty... I can't play the game but I want to get as close as I can. Anyway, anyhow.
Please, I can do this, I know I can do this.
Mum, please.

SCENE 7

1980s RUGBY GROUND

(Jean and Alex arrive at the rugby ground)

ALEX

I'm really nervous.

JEAN

You don't have to do this sweetheart.

ALEX

I want to, really want to. Just my stomach doesn't.

JEAN

Must have been my shepherd's pie.

ALEX

You think?

JEAN

I won't use the dog's food in future.

ALEX

Did ya?

JEAN

Daft bugger... the dog's food's too good for shepherd's pie.

(Enter Chairman Doug. Mike has seen them and all but hides)

There's a bloke.

ALEX

Could be any bloke.

JEAN

He looks up himself, I bet a chair is up himself, excuse me!

CHAIRMAN DOUG

Me, love?

JEAN

Chairman is it?

CHAIRMAN DOUG

That's right love.

JEAN

Right, this is my daughter who is a girl.

CHAIRMAN DOUG

Jolly good.

JEAN

But she's called Alex which sounds like a boy, even more so when it's shortened to Al which it is more often than I'd like. But Alex or Al, she is still a girl, understand?

CHAIRMAN DOUG

So far.

JEAN

Now I'm here to make sure there is no silly business when she turns up for training.

CHAIRMAN DOUG

Training?

JEAN

She knows all the rules and is as fit as a fiddle and she wants to be a ref.

CHAIRMAN DOUG

Ah ref training.

JEAN

And you said yes to her Uncle Mike, and now you can't say no to her nor laugh at her. Is that clear then?

CHAIRMAN DOUG

Mike's sister-in-law?

ALEX

My mum.

CHAIRMAN DOUG

And you're Alex?

JEAN

She is.

CHAIRMAN DOUG

Just one thing though...

ALEX

Oh Mum, I knew it!

CHAIRMAN DOUG

We can't take girls. We don't have the facilities.

JEAN

What facilities do you need for refereeing?

CHAIRMAN DOUG

Changing ones.

ALEX

I'll get changed before I come.

CHAIRMAN DOUG

Toilet ones.

ALEX

I'll go before I come.

CHAIRMAN DOUG

But if you're caught short? Sadly the lads won't like it.

JEAN

She wants to be a ref - best she gets used to not being liked.

CHAIRMAN DOUG

I wonder what your husband would say about this.

                            JEAN

You can ask him - if you're clairvoyant.

                            ALEX

We have a photo of his coffin.

                        CHAIRMAN DOUG

Ah I remember, I'm sorry -

                            ALEX

Don't be. It's a smashing coffin.

                            JEAN

Is Mike not working today?

                        CHAIRMAN DOUG

Mike got a job?

                            JEAN

I thought he was your right hand -

   (Enter Uncle Mike)

                        UNCLE MIKE

Boss! Jean! Bloody hell Jean wittering again you should learn to shut
the fuck -

                            JEAN

Watch your potty mouth in front of my daughter.

                        UNCLE MIKE

She'll need to take a bit of banter if she wants to be a ref!

                            ALEX

I fucking can and I fucking will!

                            JEAN

Alex!

                            ALEX

You said you sorted Uncle Mike!

                            JEAN

(Turning to Chairman Doug) Anything in the rules that says a girl can't
do the ref scheme?

UNCLE MIKE

Rules? *(Trying a laugh)* You're embarrassing yourself woman.

JEAN

Is there?

CHAIRMAN DOUG

I think not but -

JEAN

Wonder what the papers will make of this club not keeping its word, just 'cos she's a girl.

UNCLE MIKE

Oi! You threatening the Chairman!

CHAIRMAN DOUG

Shall we all just take it down a notch or two here. *(Pause)*
Alex?

ALEX

Yes.

CHAIRMAN DOUG

Do you really want to be a ref?

ALEX

More than anything! I love this game - this club.
Even when they lose which they do quite a lot.

CHAIRMAN DOUG

It'll be tough.

ALEX

I'm tough.

CHAIRMAN DOUG

Needs dedication.

ALEX

I'm dedicated.

CHAIRMAN DOUG

And challenging.

ALEX

I'm challenging.

CHAIRMAN DOUG

You know I think you are. Right, I said yes to your uncle even though he wasn't as clear as you Jean and Jean - we do keep our word. Alex you're in.

ALEX

Oh thank you!

CHAIRMAN DOUG

Now I best get on...
(He makes a move. Jean & Alex go. Mike starts to follow)

CHAIRMAN DOUG (CONT'D)

Mike...

UNCLE MIKE

Boss?

CHAIRMAN DOUG

Alex... is... a girl.

UNCLE MIKE

Yes Boss.

CHAIRMAN DOUG

Alex, is not a boy.

UNCLE MIKE

I... forgot?

CHAIRMAN DOUG

Quite a thing to slip even your sodden brain!
And you said that woman was in pieces!

UNCLE MIKE

She hides it well.

CHAIRMAN DOUG

Would be grateful, you said, very, very grateful!

UNCLE MIKE

She should be Boss!
She's just being a daft cow!

CHAIRMAN DOUG

That woman is not the daft one here! And if you think it's me...!
Because for a moment there...!
(Beat) Let's take it down a notch or two shall we.
The Ref Society and more importantly this club can't risk any negative
press. Anything that affects the takings.
All we need is a bunch of feminist journalists charging down here filling
their Woolworth notebooks with the word 'discrimination' underlined
exclamation mark.
We have a lot of women supporters, they know the game and we need
to keep them and more importantly get more, many more.
Things are changing Mike and our biggest challenge is controlling that
change not let the bugger control us.
I'll take the girl on, get the papers in, give her mother her photo
opportunity. I'm thinking long game, you have to in business. The kid
definitely loves this club, I'd even say needs this club, that'll be worth
a lot. Trust me.

UNCLE MIKE

I'll sort the forms, do the signing.

CHAIRMAN DOUG

That's not a job for a volunteer.

UNCLE MIKE

Volunteer?

CHAIRMAN DOUG

Volunteer. Now my car's outside, could do with a once over. Son
borrowed it again, little bugger. Would you mind.

UNCLE MIKE

—

(Exit Chairman Doug)

SCENE 8

1980s JEAN'S TERRACED HOUSE

(Alex is working out. She is doing push ups etc. Enter Jean, with a tray)

JEAN

You not ready? Ceremony starts in thirty minutes.

ALEX

I want to look good, really toned.

JEAN

You're fitter than any of them.

ALEX

Yeh, but... Is Uncle Mike coming?

JEAN

Still haven't heard from him.

ALEX

Right.

JEAN

Darl -

ALEX

No bother.

(Alex starts sit-ups or plank or something)

JEAN

Your brother's coming.

ALEX

(Pleased) Is he?

JEAN

He is.

ALEX

Dressed as Simon Le Bon?

JEAN

Think he's going more as Boy George.

ALEX

Blimey. I'm honoured.

JEAN

You are. He's been ages doing his hair. He wants to do you proud. He's really proud of you.

ALEX

Is he?

JEAN

He thinks Mike will be there and he's still coming.

ALEX

—

JEAN

You've got nothing to be nervous about. You passed top in everything.

ALEX

Yeh, I did didn't I?

JEAN

You did.

ALE

Still feels like I'm on trial.
It's not what they say it's just... it's just there. They look. You know?

JEAN

Sweetheart. You're one of the first women to be a rugby league ref for men's matches. They've got to get used to the look of you.

ALEX

I don't want to be stared at. I want to ref.

JEAN

Then just keep your head down.

ALEX

If I'd done that I wouldn't be top of my class.

JEAN

People don't like change. You have to be careful, they get...

ALEX

Careful? Keep my head down? What, are there snipers out there? Should I zig zag as well?

JEAN

You know what I mean.

ALEX

I can't 'keep my head down' or 'be careful' and be a really good ref.

JEAN

Just don't antagonise.

ALEX

Actually good advice that when faced with a 20 stone forward with a nose spread across his face. That should be in the handbook that.

JEAN

I'm just saying.

(Alex starts another exercise)

ALEX

Anyway. It's not this evening I'm bothered about, it's Monday.

JEAN

Monday?

ALEX

We get our fixture list on Monday.

JEAN

You should get good ones, being top shouldn't you?

ALEX

Yeh. Yeh I should. Maybe not all, you got to do a couple of juniors but usually... Oh Mum I just... What's that smell?

JEAN

Oh the little bugger - it's your brother at my hair spray! *(Exit Jean)*

SCENE 9

1980s CHAIRMAN'S OFFICE

(Chairman Doug and Mike are there)

CHAIRMAN DOUG

Who's next?

UNCLE MIKE

Alex.

CHAIRMAN DOUG

Last one.

UNCLE MIKE

Then you don't need me here then.

CHAIRMAN DOUG

You were with me when I told the others.

UNCLE MIKE

Yeh, but, as she's family I thought it best just coming from you. Without prejudice like.

CHAIRMAN DOUG

Without prejudice? You been reading The Guardian?

UNCLE MIKE

—

CHAIRMAN DOUG

You know Mike, you've done well recently.

UNCLE MIKE

Have I?

CHAIRMAN DOUG

Oh yes. Mike, this club is demanding Mike, very demanding, it demands a lot of me which I'm only too willing to give but it costs in more ways than one - and if you are in - fitting in - properly - way beyond volunteer - it will demand a lot of you.

(MORE)

CHAIRMAN DOUG (CONT'D)

This meeting with Alex is not going to be easy. She's not easy. I want you to think very carefully Mike as I'm afraid you might have to take sides, when she gets her list.

UNCLE MIKE

But she was top of the class.

CHAIRMAN DOUG

Oh she was, we checked the results time and time again to make sure. But decisions about her list have been made, can't be changed. If she kicks off she won't do herself any favours. The club might need your help here, Mike.

(Enter Alex)

CHAIRMAN DOUG (CONT'D)

Alex, well done love, very well done.

ALEX

Papers made me kiss the certificate. Daft eh.

CHAIRMAN DOUG

And why not? You should be right proud of yourself.

ALEX

I want to say thanks, Chairman. You gave me the opportunity to prove myself.

CHAIRMAN DOUG

And you did Alex, you did.
Here you go, love.

(Chairman Doug hands Alex an envelope. She takes it)

ALEX

Look at me shaking.

(Alex opens the envelope. She's a bit stunned)

ALEX (CONT'D)

I don't get it?

CHAIRMAN DOUG

This club doesn't sort the fixtures you know that, it's the league and others, but that's a busy few weeks you got there. The busiest I'd say - eh Mike?

ALEX

They're all the kids.
I should be getting the blokes.

CHAIRMAN DOUG

Some of them are big units.

ALEX

The others have got more than this.

CHAIRMAN DOUG

Not more, just different.
Youth teams are really important, grass roots, next generation, they need to know what good refereeing is. They need nurturing - eh Mike?

ALEX

Why can't the others nurture?

CHAIRMAN DOUG

Surely not like you? I mean you're a -

ALEX

A girl - is that it!

CHAIRMAN DOUG

No, no, no, no, no, no, let's not be defensive - eh Mike?

ALEX

I've proved I'm the best, at exams, at the physical. What's the problem?!

CHAIRMAN DOUG

No problem no it's just - Mike you tell her.

ALEX

What the fuck is it to do with him?!

UNCLE MIKE

—

CHAIRMAN DOUG

Fine. Do you really want to know love?

ALEX

Course.

CHAIRMAN DOUG

Nobody is ready for you. That's the problem.

ALEX

They should be! I'm not a novelty surprise just out of a bleeding cracker? I'll tell 'em, I'll make 'em, I'll go to the papers, TV, I'll -

CHAIRMAN DOUG

And they'll make you look hysterical. Lets take this down a notch or two eh. Listen love, you ever been to London?

ALEX

What?

CHAIRMAN DOUG

Word is, they're trying to get league going there.

ALEX

You trying to get rid of me?

CHAIRMAN DOUG

No, no, no, no, no, love, they're starting out, you're starting out, seems a good match to me.
I've got contacts down there, happy to go extra mile for you Alex.
Look, I know you're disappointed, love, I'm disappointed too, For you, for the club, but like I said we don't sort the fixtures and we never said this would be easy, now did we?

ALEX

But London. No one comes back from London.

CHAIRMAN DOUG

Don't make your mind up now. No rush. *(Showing Alex to the door)* Think on. You can let me know tomorrow.

ALEX

Tomorrow?

CHAIRMAN DOUG

League is a bit like a Sherman tank, waits for no man or woman. You have to keep one step ahead or - useful metaphor that - keeps me on my toes thinking of a Sherman tank.

In morning. First thing, let me know.

(Exit Alex. Pause)

UNCLE MIKE

I thought the Chairmen had a big say in the fixture list Boss?

CHAIRMAN DOUG

Didn't think you thought anything Mike as now't came out your bloody mouth. Why was that then?

UNCLE MIKE

—

CHAIRMAN DOUG

I don't blame her getting narked, but I do blame you for not stepping in. You still not sure which side your bread is buttered?

UNCLE MIKE

No, I mean London! Genius boss, genius!

Her mum won't like it - do you think she'll go?

CHAIRMAN DOUG

She'll be saying barrrrth and grarrse in no time.

And like she says... they don't come back from London do they?

SCENE 10

LONDON 1990s SIMON'S HOUSE

(SIMON and Alex are there. Baby crying)

> SIMON

Alex is it?

> ALEX

It is.

> SIMON

Excellent.

> ALEX

Where's the baby?

> SIMON

Piers? Upstairs. 3rd floor.

> ALEX

Attic?

> SIMON

Room next to yours.

(The baby's crying gets louder)

> SIMON (CONT'D)

He's supposed to be asleep.

> ALEX

Your wife?

> SIMON

Out. Somewhere.

> ALEX

She from our road?

SIMON

God, no.

ALEX

Where then?

SIMON

East Horley, Surrey.

ALEX

Not East Hull then?

SIMON

No.

ALEX

Not heard of the Robins?

SIMON

Only the ones who feed off the hand crafted bird house from Harrods.

ALEX

I'll go up shall I?

SIMON

She says I'm from Swanland. Not East Hull.

ALEX

Village. Outside? But you're from -

SIMON

Parents, arse licked their way to Swanland. Wall to wall personalised number plates and hand bag dogs.

It's where my dad met Chairman Doug Fletcher.

ALEX

Did he have a word?

SIMON

Sure. Dad said we needed an au pair. Doug suggested you.

ALEX

Nothing else?

SIMON

You'll want to see your room.

ALEX

Baby first.

SIMON

Oh. Course.

ALEX

The crying... Nowt wrong with him is there?

SIMON

No. We go private, so can't be.

ALEX

That's a bit...

SIMON

Bit what?

ALEX

Bit Swanland.

SIMON

(Beat) Yeh. It was. Drink? Long journey?

ALEX

In a mo.

> *(Alex exits. Simon gets drinks, pours Alex a large one. Baby stops crying. Alex returns)*

SIMON

How'd you do it?

ALEX

Do what?

                    SIMON

The crying. Stopped, like that.

                    ALEX

I cuddled him.

                    SIMON

What?

                    ALEX

He cried, I cuddled him. He's asleep.

                    SIMON

She'll go mad!

                    ALEX

For cuddling him?

                    SIMON

Best not to do it when she, Lucy, my wife, is around.

She has this book, or group, or summat, who think - dark room, let them cry, no eye contact, and definitely no cuddling and they'll be really, really happy.

Grow up to be prime ministers, bankers, that sort of thing. So if she's here just shove him in his cot, that'll be great.

                    ALEX

Do you cuddle him?

                    SIMON

(Lying) Course.

                    ALEX

—

                    SIMON

Sometimes.

                    ALEX

You were cuddled.

SIMON

You don't know that.

ALEX

Our road... somebody did.

SIMON

I had the shit kicked out of me on a regular basis down that road and nobody turned a hair.

ALEX

Maybe you were an arse that needed kicking.

SIMON

What you heard?

ALEX

C'mon some bugger cuddled you.

SIMON

Our kid. And she had to feed me, sort me for school and yes when she had time she cuddled me, parents arse licking see.

ALEX

Ahhh, sister. She in Swanland?

SIMON

When I left she married the first passing classified utter tosser, and they live in Orchard Park - no orchard and no park - that's an idiot planner's joke that is.

ALEX

You visit her?

SIMON

My wife, in Orchard Park? First sight of a pit bull and she'd be off. Anyway, business is insane. People burn out. But the rewards... I bought this house outright, on a bonus. If I'm on track - which I am - my next bonus could buy the whole of that road of yours. Why are you here?

Doug was more than a bit keen I took you.

ALEX

Was he now.

SIMON

I thought you and he... and then it went a bit... and he wanted, you know, rid.

ALEX

Doug? He's all saggy.

SIMON

But powerful, power attracts, is attractive.

ALEX

You fall for that bollocks?

SIMON

No but -

ALEX

I'm a ref.

SIMON

A what?

ALEX

Bastard! He said he had contacts! So I came all this way for what? Weird looks when I mention the weather on the underground, in a city that charges the earth for a bloody pot of Yorkshire Tea because they think it's an ethnic experience. Did that wanker say nothing!

SIMON

(Pause) Look. I might be able to...

ALEX

To what?

SIMON

This bloke at work. He's gone all professional northern tosser down here. Broadened his accent, talks rugby league bollocks loudly.

ALEX

A mate?

SIMON

He's from Lancashire.

ALEX

Right.

SIMON

Yeh. Right/ total wanker

ALEX

/Total wanker.

SIMON

But he plays somewhere with some other northern 'ex pats' as he calls 'em? Like Hampstead Heath is the bloody Costa Del Sol. But wanker or not he's supposed to be really making things happen. He's a wanker but a driven wanker. I could have a word.

ALEX

Would you?

SIMON

Course.

ALEX

Go on then! But just tell him I'm called Alex, or Al. And that I'm a ref. Got the highest score you could in ref training. Wiped the floor with the others, which I did.

SIMON

What? Don't mention the excellent...

ALEX

Funny you, straight to video.

SIMON

(Beat) It's good to have you here Al. Really good. It reminds me of...

ALEX

Why you left.

SIMON

No. What I miss.

SCENE 11

LONDON
1990s RUGBY FIELD

(Simon and WIGAN BLOKE enter Wigan Bloke is dressed in a team strip and has a captain's arm band on)

WIGAN BLOKE

Simon, mate. You got me Al, the ref?

SIMON

I certainly have mate.

WIGAN BLOKE

Thank fuck for that mate. I was bricking it. Where is he?

SIMON

The ref?

WIGAN BLOKE

Course the bloody ref!

SIMON

Getting changed in the toilets.

WIGAN BLOKE

Could have changed in the block with the blokes.

SIMON

Likes to keep/ professional distance.

WIGAN BLOKE

/Professional distance, course, course.
Mate. He is a proper ref, like not a acne ridden kid with a handbook up his arse?

SIMON

Bit intense mate. Problem?

WIGAN BLOKE

No, no, no problem.
Just. We're really trying to make league happen down here, starting to get investment, people interested, even talking to some of the pretty boy clubs - you know - union, ground share and stuff. This ref, this ref needs to be bloody shagging proper.

SIMON

And... what else?

WIGAN BLOKE

And I've got a bit of money riding on this.

SIMON

So? We bet on everything.

WIGAN BLOKE

More than a bit mate.

SIMON

How much mate?

WIGAN BLOKE

See that southern tosser over there?

SIMON

C'mon, they're wall to wall.

WIGAN BLOKE

Barbour, flat cap, checked shirt.

SIMON

Mate, you're going to have to give me a bit more.

WIGAN BLOKE

He's the one with a face like a slapped arse.

SIMON

Oh, that tosser.

WIGAN BLOKE

We were in the usual champagne bar, I was showing off to wanker proportions about how I was getting league really shifting, blah, blah bloody blah and of course he's not just a tosser, but a union tosser - so he started on about how league was rubbish and league refs were rubbish, you know/usual bollocks.

SIMON

/Usual bollocks.

WIGAN BLOKE

So I said - on your recommendation - a real mate.

SIMON

Real mate - mate.

WIGAN BLOKE

I said I could get a bloody fantastic ref who'd show him what real refereeing was and he'd have to eat his gob shite words and why doesn't he put his money where his fucking mouth is.

SIMON

And he did.

WIGAN BLOKE

But he said he wasn't pissing about for a few quid and we should make it interesting.

SIMON

How interesting?

WIGAN BLOKE

Add a fair few noughts.

SIMON

He's not from our place?

WIGAN BLOKE

No mate. He's from Enron.

SIMON

Oh shit mate!

WIGAN BLOKE

Mate, I know!

> (Enter Alex with a coat on)

SIMON

Sorted?

ALEX

Sorted. *(Wipes eyes)*

SIMON

You okay?

WIGAN BLOKE

Mate. Ref, Al. Where is he then?

> (Alex takes coat off. Pause)

WIGAN BLOKE (CONT'D)

Mate?

SIMON

Mate?

WIGAN BLOKE

Ref, mate?

SIMON

Here, mate.

WIGAN BLOKE

Is this a wind up mate? I mean is it? Cos it is fucking winding me up mate, seriously winding me up!

SIMON

Mate -

WIGAN BLOKE

I mean mate, is she even a -

SIMON

She is mate.

WIGAN BLOKE

I knew it! Bloody knew it, once a Yorkshire buggering wanker - always a - oh this is a buggering nightmare!

SIMON

Mate listen -

WIGAN BLOKE

Oh god, the union tosser is staring at me with his smug slapped arse face - I am so shafted!

SIMON

You're not thinking mate.

WIGAN BLOKE

Oh I'm thinking mate, shitting myself, but thinking.

SIMON

What do you do best mate?

WIGAN BLOKE

Mate?

SIMON

Flipping.

WIGAN BLOKE

Oh I'm bloody good at flipping.

SIMON

The best at flipping deals - apart from me.
So. Flip this.

WIGAN BLOKE

Mate I don't -?

SIMON

(To Alex) Are you one of the first female league referees ever to ref blokes games?

ALEX

I am.

SIMON

Top of the class?

ALEX

Top of the top.

SIMON

Hear that mate? North can move with the times - speeding ahead of the skanky south - top talent - that's what counts. Mate, you are a trailblazer.

WIGAN BLOKE

Trailblazer eh?

SIMON

Mate, this is the flying flip of the year!

WIGAN BLOKE

And the southern tosser can take a flying -

SIMON

He can mate, he can.

WIGAN BLOKE

Anyways, we've got no time to get another. She'll have to do, but if she stuffs up mate, I'm after your fucking arse mate and not in a good way. *(Shouting at Union bloke)* Trailblazing see! Right let's do it. Let's make this happen! Eh Simon - you and me - northern bloody powerhouse or what? Good phrase that - someone should use it. I'll get the other captain.

(Wigan Bloke starts to go)

ALEX

Hold on.

WIGAN BLOKE

Al, love - we're running late and I need to tackle some of this stress off.

ALEX

Oi! It's ref to you. And we run by my watch. Come 'ere, now!

(He does so)

ALEX (CONT'D)

(To Simon) And you.

SIMON

Me? I'm not -

ALEX

Here!

(He does so)

ALEX (CONT'D)

In future, when I've got this strip on, you will talk to me first and foremost, not any butterfly, or pretty flower or passing idiot like him that catches your attention.

SIMON

But I'm -

ALEX

Eh. I haven't finished. Secondly. When I've got this strip on you will watch your language. You know the rules and they start as soon as you and the teams see this strip. Do you understand?

(Simon and Wigan Bloke nod)

ALEX (CONT'D)

I said, do you understand?

WIGAN BLOKE

Yes Ref.

(Alex stares at Simon)

SIMON

Yes Ref.

ALEX

And thirdly, my fee has just tripled.

WIGAN BLOKE

What?!

ALEX

You 'eard, tripled. While you two were standing there with your shared brain cell straining to figure out if you were going to privilege me with the experience of keeping two lots of sweaty blokes from killing each other when there isn't another referee for miles and I mean miles 'cos I've checked, I tripled my fee.

WIGAN BLOKE

But -

ALEX

I can always walk.

WIGAN BLOKE

No, but-!

ALEX

And it will quadruple if I hear one more word of complaint. Do you understand?

WIGAN BLOKE/SIMON

(Beat) Yes, Ref.

ALEX

Pardon?

WIGAN BLOKE/SIMON

Yes Ref!

ALEX

Good. Now let's get on with the game. Get the other captain.

WIGAN BLOKE

Ref.

(Exit Wigan Bloke)

SIMON

My you're good.

ALEX

In this strip I'm invincible.

SIMON

Have you been crying?

ALEX

No. Dirt in my eye. Bloody London smog eh?

SCENE 12

LONDON
1990s RUGBY FIELD

(After match. Alex is putting on her parka coat. Enter Simon &
Wigan Bloke)

WIGAN BLOKE

That was bloody brilliant Ref, bloody brilliant!

ALEX

What? 'Cos you won.

WIGAN BLOKE

Er, slaughtered 'em!

ALEX

You did.

WIGAN BLOKE

And you were as sharp as a fucking knife.

ALEX

Eh. Language. I haven't changed yet.

WIGAN BLOKE

Can we call on you on regular basis?

ALEX

I'll check the diary.

WIGAN BLOKE

Mate, that bloke coughed up - says he was well impressed with her,
with you Ref, said you let the game flow, fierce but fair. He's thinking
he might know some backers.

SIMON

Backers? Result mate!

ALEX

Thanks. About the refereeing.

> WIGAN BLOKE

Also said you had a great pair of pins.

> ALEX

Right.

> WIGAN BLOKE

Mate.

> SIMON

Mate.

(Exit Wigan Bloke)

> SIMON (CONT'D)

He's right.

> ALEX

Great refereeing?

> SIMON

Great pair of pins.

> ALEX

Sod off.

> SIMON

Just messing. You're good at this, Al. Scary.

> ALEX

Scary?

> SIMON

But bloody good.

SCENE 13

1990s
A SOGGY PITCH SOMEWHERE IN A LONDON PARK

(Simon is waiting. Enter Al dressed as ref)

ALEX

Thanks for coming to pick me up. Not sure I'd get back from here at this time of night. Why'd they have so many midweek matches?

SIMON

Brighton.

ALEX

Brighton?

SIMON

And Bognor Regis and Hayling Island, weekend places. London empties on a Thursday. Fills up Sunday evening. Haven't you noticed?

ALEX

Always feels full to me.

SIMON

You were great.

ALEX

You watched?

SIMON

Get changed and we'll go for a swift one - to celebrate.

ALEX

I can't, Lucy said I had to get back for the baby. Think she's getting pissed off with my midweek fixtures. I don't blame her, I'm getting so many matches, maybe if she saw a match -

SIMON

She'd hate it.

ALEX

I think she hates me.

SIMON

She only just about tolerates me.

I've sorted this evening, with Lucy.

I've booked her a personal trainer for an extended session of advanced extreme yoga and Piers is doing baby 'aquatastics' at a creche my mate has just set up. He thinks he can make a killing in creches.

ALEX

Why'd you do that?

SIMON

You deserve a break, a chance to take your opportunity. A chance to celebrate it. Celebrate you.

You are really good at this. How many women are good at this? It's good to see. *(Kisses her in an ambiguous way. Beat)*

ALEX

Would you ever go back?

SIMON

To Hull? If there was good enough reason.

ALEX

Simon -

SIMON

Champagne - to celebrate.

ALEX

That's a bit -

SIMON

Are you saying no to champagne?

ALEX

Could drink you under the table. Word is you were always a lightweight.

SIMON

Only where skanky northern pub lager was involved. I was born to be drinking decent vintage bollocks. You'll see, you'll love it.

ALEX

Does Lucy love it?

SIMON

Her body is a southern temple, you'll not see a bubble pass her lips. C'mon, all the lads want to meet you.

ALEX

Lads?

SIMON

There's this champagne bar we go to after work. They'll all be there. I want them to meet you. I'm proud of you.
Want to show them what a ball-breaking scary northern lass is like.

ALEX

—

SIMON

Look. You'll have a laugh.
C'mon, let's show 'em you've bloody arrived!

SCENE 14

BAR IN LONDON. 1990s

(Enter Alex. Simon is waiting for her)

SIMON

Thank you for coming.

ALEX

Bit formal?

SIMON

Can't stay long.

ALEX

Oh?

SIMON

I'm really glad you agreed to meet up. It's been difficult I know for both of us, me working all hours - you looking after Piers and the refereeing - but you're doing brilliantly, top games -

ALEX

You been to a match recently?

SIMON

Have you eaten?

ALEX

No.

SIMON

I'll get you something. What do you want?

ALEX

You not eating?

SIMON

You look well.

ALEX

Do I?

SIMON

Very. Glowing even. Drink?
They're stupidly busy...

ALEX

You wanted to meet, about what?

SIMON

Look... about work...

ALEX

Your work?

SIMON

Your work.

ALEX

Oh?

SIMON

You've been brilliant, with Piers and everything. It's just that... you've
been different recently.

ALEX

Are you surprised?

SIMON

Lucy's noticed.

ALEX

Noticed what?

SIMON

She's worried... worried you might be different with Piers.

ALEX

Have I been?

SIMON

I'm never in to -

ALEX

Has she said I'm different?

SIMON

She says...

ALEX

What? What she say?

SIMON

You're making this difficult.

ALEX

I'll ask her shall I?

SIMON

Why do this, be like this?

ALEX

She didn't say did she?

SIMON

You're a little bit scary, you know that?

ALEX

Scary again.

SIMON

Yes. Scary, she finds you scary. I mean I can handle it but... others... others must have said?

ALEX

Oh others is it? As in your mates' others? They didn't do much saying.

SIMON

(Beat) They were drunk, stupidly drunk.

ALEX

And you?

SIMON

—

ALEX

They were your mates.

SIMON

They're not my mates. I can't control a bunch of success fueled, adrenaline fueled...

ALEX

—

SIMON

You were flirting.

ALEX

—

SIMON

Stop playing the victim.

ALEX

—

SIMON

C'mon, you didn't say no.

ALEX

I was too drunk to say yes.

SIMON

I didn't make you drink, I didn't chain you to the bar.

ALEX

It was outside the bar in the alley.

SIMON

It wasn't me.

ALEX

No. You were on the way home.

                              SIMON

I can't remember.

                              ALEX

I can.

                              SIMON

It was weeks ago.

                              ALEX

—

                              SIMON

You stayed working for me.

                              ALEX

I stayed refereeing.

                              SIMON

You want to play with the blokes? They play hard. City, Rugby League - they're all out to fuck each other.
(Beat) Lucy's pregnant. With Piers she was fine but she says she really is feeling... Maybe 'cos it's a girl. Women see, my downfall.

                              ALEX

—

                              SIMON

There's talk of China or New York at work and... I need to focus.
Look, I'm sorry but... It wasn't all bad now was it.
You've done brilliantly with your refereeing - got just what you wanted.
I'll give you two months, no three months cash, no problem.
(Beat) You are the most amazing ref.

                              ALEX

I'm not a victim.

        (Exit Alex)

SCENE 15

JEAN'S TERRACED HOUSE
1990s LIVING ROOM

(Alex stands there looking numb. Enter Jean)

JEAN

How long you staying for?

ALEX

Does it matter?

JEAN

Did I say it mattered?
Just need to know how much food to get in.

ALEX

I'll see to myself.

JEAN

No you won't you're skin and bone.

ALEX

—

JEAN

You came back quicker than...

ALEX

Down there... down there I ref'd enough serious men's matches to make their heads spin up here and I've done it brilliantly, bloody brilliantly.

JEAN

—

ALEX

Aren't you impressed? You should be.

JEAN

Course.

ALEX

Course? That it, course? Oh sorry, forgot, mustn't get above myself.

JEAN

—

ALEX

I tried to get hold of Chairman Doug - to make clear I've got more experience now than most and should get top matches up here. But you know what? Every time I rang, they said he was busy.
So I thought that Chairman Doug is trying not to see me, make me invisible - disappear.
So I thought bugger this and I went straight to the Society and the League. Straight there.
And now I have a bloody good fixture list, all blokes, that's what matters, all that matters.

JEAN

Sweetheart... I know that look.

ALEX

What look?

JEAN

In your eyes. You came back with it. *(Beat)*
My sister... One night on way home... I found her sat in the bath. She'd been there all night. Stone cold, just sat there - with that look. Said couldn't wash the smell of aftershave off.

ALEX

(Pause) Something... something did happen. But it's not - not a problem. Not anymore.

JEAN

Oh sweetheart...

(Jean goes to comfort Alex - who moves away. Jean doesn't know what to do)

JEAN (CONT'D)

I renewed your season ticket.

ALEX

Did you?

JEAN

You can pay me mind.

ALEX

Course.

JEAN

They've got a new away strip.

ALEX

I'll get it.

JEAN

It's grey.

ALEX

Grey? Why grey?

JEAN

Something about more leisure strip than sport top - can flog more they think.

ALEX

If I wear that, I'll completely disappear.

JEAN

(Beat) Do I really go on about not getting above yourself?

ALEX

You do.

JEAN

Why'd I do that then?

ALEX

—

SCENE 16

1990s CHAIRMAN'S OFFICE

(Chairman Doug is there)

CHAIRMAN DOUG

Alex! Al! How are you?

ALEX

All good. Yourself?

CHAIRMAN DOUG

Could be better - get headaches but that's the club finances -particularly with this proposed Australian tour - but, always knew it was going to be a labour of bloody love. What about you!

ALEX

What about me?

CHAIRMAN DOUG

How many men's games is it now? So many we've lost count. We knew you could do those games. We said to League and Society we said -

ALEX

I know I should, by rights, on my record, have that final. The bloke that got it has less experience than me, the blokes running the lines are less experienced than me, so why don't I Doug?

CHAIRMAN DOUG

Honestly Alex?

ALEX

You and the other chairmen not ready?

CHAIRMAN DOUG

It's not just the chairmen.

ALEX

We all know this is a club game, the clubs run the game. The Chair - men run the game.

CHAIRMAN DOUG

It's not about men or women it's about rugby. It was a rugby decision.

ALEX

Decided on what!? Fuck sake I nailed Filey!

CHAIRMAN DOUG

Shall we take this down a notch or two.

ALEX

Shall we not Doug.
I'm going to Society - League - one door won't have a foot behind it.

CHAIRMAN DOUG

Listen, you ever been to Australia?

ALEX

Australia.

CHAIRMAN DOUG

I put an idea forward - levered it - to the Society - to League - cheeky idea - backing you - and they ran with it. Agreed to pay for you to go to Australia.

ALEX

Transport me? For what, being criminally good at refereeing whilst in charge of a pair of breasts?

CHAIRMAN DOUG

You know this club is touring. Pre-season friendly.

ALEX

Course.

CHAIRMAN DOUG

Go with them.
You can take in the antipodean refereeing atmosphere.

ALEX

Ref a game?

CHAIRMAN DOUG

Yeh, try and get a game. Not on the tour, that's all sorted, but there's bound to be other games in the outback. See we - the club - the Society League - want to support you, nurture you, by making sure you are absolutely ready.

ALEX

For a final?

CHAIRMAN DOUG

Australia. Land of opportunity. Have a think. Don't linger though, you want change quick. So best get thinking. This afternoon, for an answer, yes?

ALEX

No.

CHAIRMAN DOUG

No?

ALEX

You can have it now, my answer. A bit fat bloody yes. Like you say Doug, Australia, land of opportunity.

(Alex leaves)

SCENE 17

AUSTRALIA RUGBY PITCH. 2000s

(KEV is there in shirt sleeves. He is busy - distracted. Enter Alex in ref outfit)

                    ALEX

S'cuse me?

                    KEV

Pommie?

                    ALEX

Sharp you.

                    KEV

Ref's British. I'm supposed to meet him here. Got to warn him.

                    ALEX

And you are?

                    KEV

Kev. Kev Kopec. Manage the club. Not players, just the club.

   (He turns. Sees Alex, clocks the ref outfit)
You... got something in your eye?

                    ALEX

Just sweat.

                    KEV

You're -

                    ALEX

The ref.
Alex. Al if you like.

                    KEV

They didn't say -

ALEX

What should they have said Kev?
What they did say to me Kev was that this was a grudge match.

KEV

I was going to say, to the ref to -

ALEX

To me, Alex - the ref. Get used to it in your mouth Kev. Roll it round on your tongue like a gob full of your fine Australian lager.

KEV

This is not just any grudge match.
These guys are usually rational controlled professionals but we had six sent off last time, three on stretchers and one of those was a Touch Judge. Usually the bloke - ref - in the middle has been round the block.

ALEX

I've refereed more grudge matches - we call them derbies, god knows why - more derbies than you got kangaroos in this country Kev.

        (Enter Captain Steve)

CAPTAIN STEVE

Eh, Kev! Has the Ref rocked up?

KEV

Steve Morrow, the club -

ALEX

Captain Steve Morrow, one hundred and forty appearances for club and six for country. Word is it should have been more but for suspect hamstring.

CAPTAIN STEVE

(Beat) I don't believe it!

KEV

Steve -

CAPTAIN STEVE

I know you!

KEV

You do?

CAPTAIN STEVE

Course I bloody do! She's the woman who ref'd Filey!
My uncle saw it, said you didn't put a foot wrong.

KEV

That you?

ALEX

Uhuh.

CAPTAIN STEVE

(Shouting to his team) Oi. She may be a bloody Pom but she's the one
did bloody Filey! Yeh! Bloody Filey!

ALEX

Okay now, if we have finished our bit of banter, let's get back to basics.
For the sake of Commonwealth relations there will be no bloody
swearing in any language - Aussie or English - when I'm wearing this
rather damp strip and holding this whistle understand?

CAPTAIN STEVE

My uncle, he'll want your autograph.

ALEX

I said understand!

CAPTAIN STEVE & KEV

Yes Ref.

SCENE 18

AUSTRALIA. 2000s LEAGUE CLUB PUB

(Loud music. Kev has a drink, enjoying the music. Enter Alex)

ALEX

This league club pub is huge!

KEV

Normal Aussie water hole. Schooner?

ALEX

You what?

KEV

Beer - lager?

ALEX

No thanks.

KEV

Don't drink?

ALEX

Allergic to bubbles.

KEV

Oh right - well have what I'm having. *(Hands her a red wine)*
Don't underestimate the Aussie capacity for making a damn fine wine.
It's in the DNA and it's supposed to be good for the heart.

ALEX

The heart eh. Just one. *(Takes drink)*

KEV

Me too. Goes to my head a bit.
You did good. Only two off and those on stretchers. No cards shown,
flowing game.

ALEX

I did, didn't I?

                    KEV

What you doing here?

                    ALEX

Refereeing.

                    KEV

How long you staying?

                    ALEX

As long as I'm refereeing.

                    KEV

Nothing to go back to?

                    ALEX

If you'd known I was a woman... before the match?

                    KEV

Don't underestimate the Aussie capacity to just get on with it. It's in the DNA.
Look, over here we are impressed with anyone who excels at what they do. Out there you were always in charge, complete professional.

                    ALEX

Do you find me scary?

                    KEV

Scary? I find funnel web spiders scary. Red back snakes scary and my tax return scary. But you... why should I find you scary?

    (Black Box 'Right on Time' comes on)

                    ALEX

Oh I love this!

                    KEV

Blimey, me too!

                    ALEX

Can you dance?

KEV

Don't underestimate the Aussie capacity to be crap at dancing.

ALEX

It's in their DNA?

KEV

No just mine.

ALEX

Mine too!

(Alex starts to dance and sing badly at the same time)

SCENE 19

AUS. CHANGING ROOM. 2000s

(Crying, wailing silently. She gathers herself. Wipes her nose on her sleeve like a snotty kid)

ALEX

A cup final.
Not any cup final.
A bloody Australian cup final and me.
In the middle.
Me.
I've arrived. Bloody arrived. Mind you, On other side of the world.

(Blows nose, wipes eyes. Enter Kev)

KEV

You okay?

ALEX

Course.

KEV

It's just your eyes are...

ALEX

They cleaned in here with bleach?
Sets me off something rotten smell of bleach.

KEV

You do this every time - the crying.

ALEX

Oh Kev, what if I stuff up?

KEV

You won't.

ALEX

There's a lot at home who would love me to stuff up.

KEV

Stuff 'em, you won't.

ALEX

Everything is so simple for you Aussies.

KEV

It is simple. You got this, the final, because you are more than good enough.

ALEX

I did didn't I?

KEV

Not just top of he class, top of the bloody game.

(Exit Kev)

ALEX

I love this game. The true game. It makes you feel you belong, whatever bloody genitals you were born with.
Whistle (Checks)
Watch (Checks)
Cards? (Checks)

KEV

(Off) You ready Ref?

ALEX

Never been more ready.

(End of Act One)

ACT TWO

SCENE 20

AUS. 2000s CHANGING ROOM

(Alex is lying there on a stretcher. She is obviously in a lot of pain. It's her knee. It's wrapped in ice. Enter Kev)

ALEX

Is it swelling up?

KEV

A bit.

ALEX

How much?

KEV

A little.

ALEX

How much?

KEV

Like a hot air balloon, but a really big one.

(He puts more ice on it. Alex yells in pain)

KEV (CONT'D)

It's ice - just ice.

ALEX

Jesus wept, sixty bloody minutes.

KEV

You did brilliantly.

ALEX

What was he thinking?

KEV

He wasn't even looking let alone thinking, too pumped, there's always one.

ALEX

He bloody tackled me! The bloody ref! Has he played the bloody game before?

KEV

He wants to see you, say sorry.

ALEX

If he bloody comes in here, I'll bloody red card him! *(She moves)* Argh!

KEV

Stay still, the ambulance is coming.

ALEX

Why?

KEV

Why? Your leg... is not right.

ALEX

What you mean not right?

KEV

As in, it's all wrong.

ALEX

The ice will sort it.

KEV

—

ALEX

Kev. You said it was swollen - just swollen.

KEV

Did I?

ALEX

KEV!

KEV

Your knee... it's not where it should be.

ALEX

Is it not?

KEV

No.

ALEX

Where is it then?

KEV

Where it shouldn't be.

ALEX

You seen this sort of knee before?

KEV

Yes.

ALEX

Often?

KEV

(Beat) No.

ALEX

You could have lied.

KEV

I did. I haven't seen this before ever.

ALEX

You look kind of...

KEV

Do I?

ALEX

You do.

KEV

Probably because I'm going to have to go and throw up.

(Exit Kev)

ALEX

Bloody Natalia Barbiecov - got your bloody revenge. You spiteful dog chewed Barbie bitch.

SCENE 21

JEAN'S TERRACED HOUSE. 2000s

(Alex is sitting with her leg heavily strapped, drinking. She has been there for a while. Enter Jean. She busies herself folding washing. She notices Alex is drinking. She folds clothes with disapproval. Alex begins to notice)

ALEX

Do you have to?

JEAN

Do I have to what?

ALEX

I know what you're doing.

JEAN

I'm not doing anything.

ALEX

Yes you are. You know you are.

JEAN

Washing doesn't get folded by itself.

ALEX

Yeh, right, you are folding them in 'that way'.

(Jean pauses for a moment then continues to fold with disapproval. In response Alex pours herself a huge drink)

JEAN

How many is that?

ALEX

Don't judge me.

JEAN

I just asked.

                    ALEX

You asked in 'that way'.

                    JEAN

What way is that?

                    ALEX

That 'judging way'.

                    JEAN

What 'judging' way?

                    ALEX

That 'you've been drinking since breakfast' judging way.

                    JEAN

Have you?

                    ALEX

—

                    JEAN

Well?

                    ALEX

Mebe.

                    JEAN

Oh Alex...

                    ALEX

Don't you 'oh Alex' me.

                    JEAN

There's no talking to you -

                    ALEX

How would you know? You ever try?

                    JEAN

I'm just saying -

ALEX

The problem is you don't say, you just look in 'that way' and do the 'oh' thing and fold the washing with a massive 'munk' on.

JEAN

Your drinking is not -

ALEX

I'm in training. I aim to retain my record of being able to drink any bloke under the table.

JEAN

You're practising enough.

ALEX

Ladies and gentleman motherly love has just left the building.

(Jean does something with the washing)

ALEX (CONT'D)

That s'posed to make me feel bad?

'Cos I tell you, the bugger who did my knee has beaten you hands down.

JEAN

Look you've messed up your knee and I'm sorry about that. You can't referee anymore and I'm sorry about that. Sorry but -

ALEX

Sorry but? Sorry but! Is that the best you can do? You never wanted me to do refereeing - never.

JEAN

I took you!

ALEX

'Do they know she's a she?' 'I'm not having a child of mine laughed at.' Well they're all bloody laughing now.

But you know what Jean, least I had a go. I made something happen, you just let life happen to you.

JEAN

Don't do this -

ALEX

What you ever done eh? What? Oh yeh. A job going nowhere and a crap marriage. And what else?

Let's see - oh yeh - a big fat nothing - that's what.

But at least they can't laugh at you.

Mind you that's 'cos they can't hear you or see you - invisible bloody woman you.

JEAN

I brought you two up!

ALEX

Oh - yeh - Steve puts more illegal stuff up his nose than a boy band and according to you I'm on the way to having a liver like an exotic sea sponge from Harvey Nichols -

JEAN

Excuse me, but Steven has got a part in Priscilla Queen of the Desert on tour. It's speaking - he has two whole lines.

ALEX

Well let's hope he doesn't bugger his knee in the dance sequences - that would be bloody ironic - your daughter buggers hers on a rugby pitch, your son buggers his in high heels and a tiara sashaying backwards whilst miming to Abba. A triumph of parenting that.

JEAN

Oh, Alex, don't -

ALEX

'Oh' Alex? 'Oh' 'oh', 'oh'!
Did you do the 'oh' thing to Dad? Is that why he got in that car in 'that way' with 'that -

JEAN

Course I did. I put him in that car with that permed floozy and jumped up and down in glee on the accelerator.

(MORE)

JEAN (CONT'D)

Last thing he heard was me cackling hysterically as they hit the silver birch at speed. It's amazing what you can do when you're the invisible woman!

(Pause)

ALEX

I love the game. I wanted to be part of... I worked harder than anyone else to... belong.

I got close, but only as close as they would let me.

(Beat) They've won haven't they?

(Pause)

JEAN

You're right.

ALEX

—

JEAN

About me.

You and Steven. Both brave and beautiful and wonderfully gobby. You were the best thing. The best thing I ever did - ever.

And what do I do to my best achievement? Tell you not to get above yourself - I've thought so long and hard about that Darl.

See I thought the difference between your Dad and me - he wanted you both to be like him - but me - oh not like me - or him come to that.

And then I come out with that silly stupid rubbish.

I got scared Darl, so bloody scared. And I faded and faded and faded till I was scared to look in the mirror in case I wasn't there.

Darl. Don't you fade, please don't fade.

ALEX

But I've tried to play their game -

JEAN

Yes, their game. So don't.

ALEX

But they own the game.

JEAN

Not true league, the game you love.

ALEX

But - my knee - Mum - I'm broken.

JEAN

Have you come this far, just to come this far?

You've learnt so much, know so much. Sweetheart. We'll mend you and then you need to get above yourself, high, high, high above yourself. And then you can shit on Chairman Doug from a great height

(Pause)

ALEX

When did you get so bloody wise?

JEAN

Being invisible. Means you can hang out in libraries, theatres, the occasional council meeting, even a mixed sauna. As long as you don't wear too floral a perfume, but it's amazing what you can glean.

SCENE 22

RUGBY CLUB. 2000s

(Chairman Doug is there unsettled. Enter Alex. She limps)

CHAIRMAN DOUG

Alex.

ALEX

Doug.

CHAIRMAN DOUG

Still crocked?

ALEX

Getting better.

CHAIRMAN DOUG

Really? Cruciate ligament I hear?

ALEX

It is but -

CHAIRMAN DOUG

Nasty, very nasty. If you were an animal they'd put you down.

ALEX

—

CHAIRMAN DOUG

Ha! Just a little -

Shame about cup final eh! You get there in the middle and then - but at least you experienced part of one even if it was Australian.

ALEX

League here - looking more and more towards Australia.

CHAIRMAN DOUG

But with your knee now - you had a good run Alex - no pun intended - you gave it a good go and she did her best by you.

ALEX

She?

CHAIRMAN DOUG

The club. She can be a bitch of a she-devil but -

ALEX

I've got a letter for you.

(Holds out letter)

CHAIRMAN DOUG

For me?

(Takes letter)

ALEX

For you.
It's the outcome of several meetings I've had with the Society, the League.

CHAIRMAN DOUG

Several?

(Starts to read letter)

ALEX

The letter, more of a brief really, explains it fully.

CHAIRMAN DOUG

This is...

ALEX

Clean sweep, new broom I think it says.

You see back from Australia with my leg up I did a lot of thinking.

I thought how I'd worked really hard at being a ref your way, played your game - best in year and after, yet strangely, no cup final.

And I thought, do I keep banging my head against your firmly shut doors with your foot firmly jammed behind it?

And I thought, I'd probably get brain damage like that and end up like an ex player who's taken one too many tackles to the head. So what to do?

CHAIRMAN DOUG

I understand with the knee you might feel bitter but this is -

ALEX

Bitter was only the half of it Doug.

I tell you, lying there with my knee in pieces I thought, there's no fixing me or them.

And I felt bitter and a little bit sorry for myself. And I wondered about crawling away - 'cos I couldn't bloody walk - and becoming really, really quiet. Defeated Doug.

CHAIRMAN DOUG

(Indicating letter) But this...

ALEX

And then I thought. Bugger this.

I'm not going to go around wearing a grey second strip for leisure purposes only, I want a fluorescent team strip with lots of logos.

If I can't fix them, I'll step over them. That letter there - that's change.

CHAIRMAN DOUG

If it ain't broke don't fix it.

ALEX

Oh it's broke alright Doug, but broke suits you.

As you can see from the letter they have placed me in charge with full financial backing - of two significant new projects, one of which is the revamping of the Referee Training Scheme, the other is a Women's Rugby League World Cup.

CHAIRMAN DOUG

What? Women playing?

ALEX

Oh yes.

To be clear, the ref training programme will be run, transparently. It will have a series of transparent national training guidelines which key in to transparent international guidelines and it will be run transparently by the Ref Society alone and not by the clubs.

(MORE)

ALEX (CONT'D)

Did you notice how often I said transparent Doug. Because interestingly during my meetings with the Society and the League it became clear how lacking in transparency decision making has been, particularly in relation to the awarding of games and cup finals. But you know all about those decisions don't you Doug as it seems you were pretty instrumental in the making of them. Making sure I didn't get a cup final.

(Beat)

CHAIRMAN DOUG

You and me Alex, we're not that different.

This club - she was a constant. Whatever shit was being thrown at me as a kid out there - and there was a lot of it - I felt... The club was always there for me. I'll be transparent with you. It saved me. And I vowed, I'd be there for the club. See, not that different eh. Eh?

ALEX

—

CHAIRMAN DOUG

And when I started making my way, earning a bit - a bloody sight more than a bit - when I did, and could give something back - it was never disabled children or cancer charities for me. Let someone else look like a prat shaking a tin in the draught of a supermarket automatic door. No.

It was always going to be doing whatever I can for this girl, always.

Now there are some at the top table of this business, they don't love the clubs.

They love projects like the ones you've come up with 'cos they believe it's another tick in the box - their box mind - that has OBE written on it.

You'll do the projects, they'll take the credit.

Look, you love this club almost as much as I do. I saw it in you the first day you came here. Don't bother with stuff that's just going to get someone else a gong. Come back here, help the club.

ALEX

Doing what?

CHAIRMAN DOUG

I'll find you something. There's always something needs doing. Your knees buggered which is problematic but not insurmountable - we've taken the seriously damaged back into the fold before, look at your Uncle Mike.

(He sees that as a joke. Alex does not)

ALEX

What job Doug?

CHAIRMAN DOUG

Bit of this, bit of that, cleaning is out of the question with your knee, but that's detail we'll sort later.

Drop the projects, Alex, come back to the club, the club that's done so much for you. I mean London, remember?

ALEX

You did make London happen, didn't you Doug?

CHAIRMAN DOUG

And then Australia, I worked hard to get you to Australia.

ALEX

Oh you did, you did.

CHAIRMAN DOUG

To be honest, I'm not grateful about much. I worked bloody hard to get where I am. But I'm really grateful I can be there for this big beautiful bitch of a club, bloody grateful. And you know, you should be too, very, very grateful.

ALEX

(Beat) You didn't think I'd come back. Did you Doug. London, Australia. I'm going to do those projects and do them bloody well and neither will be connected to you or this club.

(Pause)

CHAIRMAN DOUG

So, you choose to go with the fly boys. History repeating itself eh? Seems you've always been taken with fly boys. Simon told me about London. Did you go with the fly boys in Australia too eh? Buggered your knee entertaining them?

I mean how long do you think they'll be interested eh?

I'm just being really honest here Alex when I say you're not exactly poster material are you, they're not going to want to put you on show as the face of the projects and when you have a few drinks, women are ugly when they drink and I hear you're no exception.

They'll soon want to forget you. Shut the door in your face.

Invisible woman you. Another victim of a couple of politically correct projects that were never meant to succeed, not really.

ALEX

This club is not a bitch, a tart, a girl or a she in any form.

This club houses the beautiful game - THE beautiful game - the true game of league, not your poisoned version.

CHAIRMAN DOUG

It wouldn't survive without people like me.

ALEX

It's not a game for a few dinosaurs like yourself Doug. I mean you are a true and accurate depiction of a dinosaur - David Attenborough has probably done a mini series on you.

The truly beautiful game makes people feel they belong, involved, playing, watching, taking tickets or making sausage rolls with pig tails and they are all, all, all bloody valued for it.

I'm so glad I went to Australia Doug. It was there I figured out that I'm not scared of people like you, don't have to try and please you. And I'm not scary to anyone with more than a shrivelled prune for a soul.

I'm a brilliant, triumphant, truly amazing survivor. And you know what survivors do, when one door is shut in their face, foot jammed behind it? They open another one. That's what doors do Doug. They shut, but they open too.

And now Doug - to demonstrate I'm going to open that door and walk through it. And any other door that is shut to me. Not invisible me, Doug. Not anymore.

SCENE 23

JEAN'S TERRACED HOUSE

(Alex and Jean are humming something remembered. Peaceful)

> ALEX

You ever see Uncle Mike?

> JEAN

Not since the kerfuffle.

> ALEX

What kerfuffle?

> JEAN

I was out, Mike came round.

> ALEX

Who was in?

> JEAN

Steve.

> ALEX

How'd you know there was a kerfuffle? Steve say?

> JEAN

By Steve's knuckles.

> ALEX

Mike attack Steve?

> JEAN

Seems that Mike was really pissed even for him. Steve answered the door in a dress.

> ALEX

Oh.

JEAN

He was practising - the heels they have to wear are so high, I don't know how he does it.

ALEX

Did Mike get arsey?

JEAN

Not exactly.

ALEX

So what exactly?

JEAN

He asked to try the dress on.

ALEX

Oh? And did Steve let him?

JEAN

He did.

ALEX

Oh. Did the colour suit?

JEAN

Steve said the colour did but the silk seams were screaming at the size of his beer belly. But when he asked Mike to take it off he wouldn't.

ALEX

Oh.

JEAN

Said he'd been dying to put one on for years. Wanted to keep it on. Started dancing round the room.

ALEX

Drunk Uncle dancing?

JEAN

He got quite vicious - 'bout dress.

In the end Steve said fine Mike could keep it on but he had to go home – wearing it.

Mike started on about Steve flaunting it and why did he have to show off and how your dad made sure Mike never showed off by regularly giving him a right smacking and maybe he should do the same to Steve. Thing is, with all his dancing Steve is really fit now. So he picked Mike up - Mike squirming like a demented spider - and threw him out with the dress still on - into the street. He had to walk past the Co-op like that with those big windows. And it was busy.

                              ALEX

Oh!

                              JEAN

Yes oh!
(Pause) Will I like him?

                              ALEX

Dunno, will you?

                              JEAN

What's he called?

                              ALEX

Kev.

                              JEAN

That's not Australian. There's a Kev 'round the corner.

                              ALEX

It is now.

                              JEAN

(Beat) Will he like me?

                              ALEX

Will he not?

                              JEAN

(Beat) Will he like Steven?

ALEX

Kev... His music collection in car...

JEAN

Yes?

ALEX

Got the sound track of Priscilla Queen of the Desert.

JEAN

Does he now?

ALEX

He does.

JEAN

Steve has got a main part in it now. The one Graham Norton did.

ALEX

Has he now?

JEAN

He has. *(Beat)* I didn't know Graham Norton was gay.

ALEX

Did you not?

JEAN

Just well groomed. *(She hums then -)* How long he staying?

ALEX

Dunno.

JEAN

You must have some idea.

ALEX

Till the work stops?

JEAN

What work.

ALEX

Consultancy.

JEAN

Consulting with who?

ALEX

Me.

JEAN

Right.

ALEX

Yeh. Yeh, it is.